Take-Home Books
Grade 2

Harcourt

Orlando   Boston   Dallas   Chicago   San Diego

Visit *The Learning Site!*
www.harcourtschool.com

Contents

TAKE-HOME BOOK
Something New
Use with "Lucy's Quiet Book."

Answers:

_2_ Grandma had an idea.

_4_ Jake read to Sally.

_3_ Jake and Grandma read together.

_1_ Jake got home and opened his book.

Fold

Jake Can Read

by Betsy Franco
illustrated by Bob Dellinger

Jake's Book

Show what happened in *Jake Can Read*. Copy each sentence and blank on its own sheet of paper. Write 1, 2, 3, and 4 to put them in order. Then draw a picture for each sentence. (Turn the page to find the answers.)

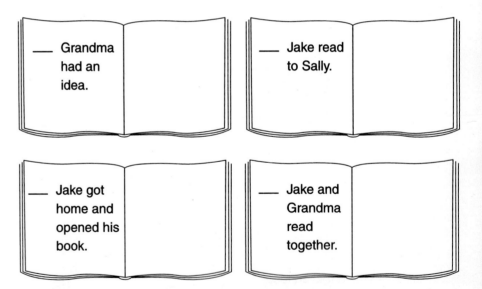

___ Grandma had an idea.

___ Jake read to Sally.

___ Jake got home and opened his book.

___ Jake and Grandma read together.

 School-Home Connection Ask your child to read Jake Can Read to you. Then ask what books your child enjoys reading or listening to.

"I'll read to you, Sally," said Jake.

"Then, when you get bigger, we'll read together. I'll read one page, and you'll read the next!"

12

Jake had to read a book for homework.

He found a book to read.

"I wonder if I will like this book," Jake thought.

1

Jake got home and opened his book.

He read page one.

He could not read all of page two.

"I need help reading this book,"

he said.

Jake started to read a lot.

Sometimes he read by himself.

Sometimes he read with Grandma.

Then one day, he had an idea.

"I can read to Sally," Jake said.

One day, Grandma was not home.

Jake read a book all by himself!

He grinned.

When Grandma came home, she
grinned, too.

Jake heard loud sounds.

His sister was playing and having fun.

That made Jake a little angry.

He did not want to read.

He wanted to be loud like Sally.

Jake's grandma came into the room.

Grandma saw Jake with his book.

"Are you reading?" she asked.

"Do you like your book?"

4

Every day, Jake and Grandma read together.

They started with short books.

Soon the books got longer.

Jake was surprised.

"I like reading," he said. "Reading is fun!"

9

Jake read page one. Grandma read page two.

Then Grandma helped Jake with page three.

Jake grinned. He was surprised.

He was having fun, and he wasn't angry anymore.

8

"I want to play, Grandma," said Jake.

"I do not want to read. This is a hard book."

"Maybe I can help you, Jake," Grandma said.

5

"I have an idea, Jake," Grandma said.

"What's your idea, Grandma?"
Jake said.

"We can read your book together,"
she said.

6

Jake took the book and sat by Grandma.

"I wonder if this will be fun," he thought.

"I wonder if this will be fun," Grandma
thought.

Then they started to read.

7

TAKE-HOME BOOK
Something New
Use with "Henry and Mudge Under the Yellow Moon."

Answers: 1. T   2. F   3. F   4. T   5. T   6. T   7. T   8. T

Fold

Chipmunks Do What Chipmunks Do

by Julie Verne
illustrated by Laurel Aiello

All About Chipmunks

On a sheet of paper, write the numbers 1 to 8. Read the sentences below. If the sentence tells something true, write a T. If the sentence tells something not true, or false, write an F. (Turn the page to find the answers.)

1. Chipmunks can wake up in the winter.

2. Chipmunks go south for the winter.

3. Chipmunks do not save food for winter.

4. Chipmunks eat nuts and seeds.

5. Bears sleep in caves in winter.

6. Chipmunks sleep underground in the winter.

7. Chipmunks carry nuts in their cheeks.

8. Raccoons sleep in trees.

 School-Home Connection Invite your child to read *Chipmunks Do What Chipmunks Do* to you. Then ask your child to find a picture in the book and tell what is happening in it.

Do you ever see chipmunks in fall?

Now you will know what they are doing.

Chipmunks do what chipmunks do!

12

What do chipmunks do in the fall?

Chipmunks don't do what other animals do.

Chipmunks are chipmunks.

Chipmunks do what chipmunks do.

1

Chipmunks aren't like bears.
They don't sleep in caves.
Chipmunks aren't like raccoons.
They don't sleep in trees.
Chipmunks do what chipmunks do.

Chipmunks sleep almost all winter long.
Sometimes the winter sun warms the ground.
The chipmunks may wake up to eat.
Then they go back to sleep.

Winter is here.

It's time for chipmunks to sleep in their underground nests.

That's what chipmunks do when the cold winter comes.

10

Chipmunks always know when it is fall.

The trees turn red and yellow.

Chipmunks watch leaves drop from trees.

They know when the days get shorter.

3

Chipmunks spend time sniffing the air in the woods.

The air feels colder.

It smells like fall to the chipmunks.

They know that winter is coming.

The chipmunks are no longer sniffing the air. They have picked up and saved their food.

The bears are in their caves.

The raccoons are in the trees.

The fish are under the water.

The birds have gone south.

Birds fly south for the winter, but chipmunks don't go south.

They stay in the woods.

Chipmunks don't do what birds do.

Chipmunks do what chipmunks do.

The woods have a lot of food for chipmunks.

The chipmunks gather the food.

They pack their cheeks with it.

Then they save the food for winter.

The best foods to save are nuts and seeds.

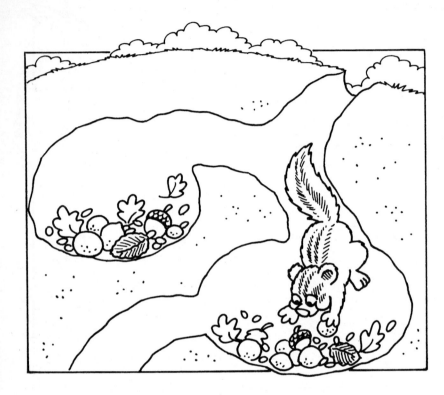

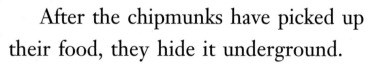

After the chipmunks have picked up
their food, they hide it underground.

That is where chipmunks go in winter.

Chipmunks sleep underground when
winter comes.

6

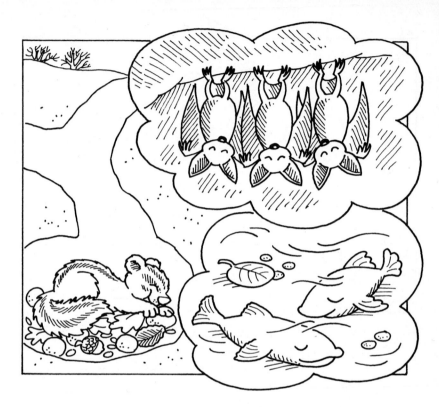

Chipmunks aren't like brown bats.

They don't find a cave.

Chipmunks aren't like fish.

They don't stay underwater.

Chipmunks are chipmunks.

They sleep under the ground.

7

TAKE-HOME BOOK
Something New
Use with "Days With Frog and Toad."

Answers should include some of the following: reading alone or with
a family member; playing in a meadow alone or with friends; building
with blocks alone; going on a seesaw with a friend; thinking alone;
playing baseball, tag, or hide-and-seek with friends; being at a party
with friends; playing with a special toy alone.

Fold

Alone Time, Together Time

by Jesse Levine
illustrated by Ruth J. Flanigan

Story Time

Tell about the story. On a sheet of paper, write two things that the story says are fun to do alone. Then write two things that are fun to do together with friends. (Turn the page to find the answers.)

Alone   Together

School-Home Connection Ask your child to read *Alone Time, Together Time* to you. Then talk about the things each of you likes to do alone and with others for fun.

Fold

It's fine to be alone.
It's fine to be together.
Both are fine, and both are fun.

What is a good reason to do something alone?

Doing something alone can be fun.
What do you like to do alone?

What is a good reason to do something with friends or family?

Doing something together can be fun.

What do you like to do together with your friends or family?

It's fun to be with your friends at your birthday party.

You can play games together.

It's fun to be alone after your birthday party.

You can play with something special.

Sometimes it's nice to be together
with friends.

You can play games like baseball or tag
or hide-and-seek.

You can cheer up friends who are sad.

Do you like to read books?

It is fun to read alone.

On rainy days, you might read all
day long.

Reading alone is a fine way to spend a
rainy day.

It is fun to read together.

A family member might read to you at bedtime.

Reading together is a fine thing to do before you go to sleep.

4

Sometimes it's nice to be alone because it's quiet.

You can think about what you want to be when you grow up.

You can think about things you have seen and done.

9

Sometimes you can be having fun together.

Then your fun is spoiled.

Maybe your friend has to go home.

Now you are alone, so you can't go on the seesaw!

8

It is fun to play alone in a meadow.
You can hear birds and feel grass.
You can look up to see clouds.
You can look down to see tiny bugs.
Playing alone in my meadow is a fine way to have fun.

5

It is fun to play with friends in a
meadow.

You can play tag together.

You can look at the clouds and tell
stories about what you see.

Playing together in our meadow is a
fine way to have fun.

6

Sometimes you can be having fun
alone.

Then your fun is spoiled when your
dog wants to be with you.

Maybe it wants you to cheer it up.

Now you are together, but your block
house is spoiled!

7

TAKE-HOME BOOK
Something New
Use with "Wilson Sat Alone."

Answers: Jenny wished for a baby sister. Children could draw
Jenny and Jamie playing ball, playing in the yard, going for a walk,
or sleeping.

Fold

Jenny's Wish

by Ted Jamison
illustrated by Claude Martinot

Star Light, Star Bright

Jenny wished the same wish every night. What was her wish? On a sheet of paper, draw one big star and write your answer in it. Then draw pictures in two smaller stars to show two things Jenny did when her wish came true. (Turn the page to find the answers.)

 School-Home Connection Have your child read *Jenny's Wish* to you. Then ask your child what wish he or she would make on a star.

Fold

Then Jenny would remember her wish.
She would give Jamie a big hug.
Jenny was very glad to have Jamie.
She had gotten her wish on a star!

Jenny had a room with a window.
At night she liked to watch the stars
clustered in groups in the sky.
Jenny also liked to look for planets.
She wondered if another girl was
looking out her window at stars and
planets, too.

Each night Jenny wished on a star.
  Star light, star bright,
  First star I see tonight.
  I wish I may, I wish I might,
  Have the wish I wish tonight.
Each night Jenny wished the same wish.

2

Sometimes Jamie spoiled Jenny's toys.
She colored on them.

  Sometimes Jamie bumped into Jenny's
books. They fell onto the rug.

  Sometimes Jenny wished that she had
her room to herself.

11

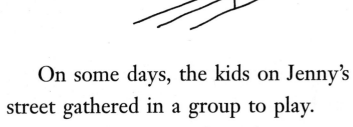

Jenny liked to take Jamie for walks.

They always wandered down the street.

Then they wandered back home together.

10

On some days, the kids on Jenny's street gathered in a group to play.

Jenny always raced up the street with them and then back down again.

Then she went home alone.

On those nights, Jenny wished her same wish.

3

On some days, Jenny's friends came to her house to play.

Jenny and her friends always had fun playing games.

Then Jenny's friends went home.

On those nights, Jenny wished her same wish.

4

Jamie got bigger.

Jenny played with her outside.

They raced around the yard together.

Jenny always hid in a new spot.

Jamie looked around until she found Jenny.

9

Every day Jenny gathered together
Jamie's toys.

She made groups of toys all around
the room.

Then she would ask Jamie to choose
one of the groups.

Jenny and Jamie played with those toys.

8

On some nights, Jenny, Mom, and Dad
gathered in Jenny's room.

They raced her toy cars and had fun.

Then Mom and Dad said "Good
night," and Jenny got into bed.

On those nights, Jenny wished her
same wish.

5

Then one day, Jenny's wish came true.

She got a baby sister named Jamie!

Mom, Dad, and Jenny gathered around
the baby's crib.

Jenny grinned.

She wasn't alone in her room anymore!

6

Jamie's crib stayed in Jenny's room.

At night Jenny always showed Jamie the
stars clustered in the sky.

Then Jenny found the brightest star.

"I wished on that star for you," she
told Jamie.

7

TAKE-HOME BOOK
Something New
Use with "The Mixed-Up Chameleon."

Answers:
Children may draw any of the following animals:
lizard
snake
frog
birds
crab
butterfly
deer
bugs
turtle

Fold

Hiding Places

by Betsy Franco
illustrated by Kees de Kiefte

Hidden Animals

Draw a picture of the woods and marsh. Show three of the animals the children saw on their hike. Then trade pictures with a classmate. Write each animal's name beside its picture. (Turn the page to find possible answers.)

School-Home Connection Invite your child to read *Hiding Places* to you. Then ask your child what bugs or animals might be hiding in your backyard.

We thought we would be alone in the woods, but we aren't.

Our hike is exciting because we spot many animals.

I wonder how many animals spot us.

12

Jim and I are in the woods by the marsh behind our house.

At first, we think there are hardly any animals around us.

Then we find out that there are hiding places everywhere.

1

A tree frog hides on the bark of a tree.

The frog is a dull-brown color, so it
hides on the dull-brown bark.

It is hard to see the frog there.

Look at us.

We are not hard to spot in our red
shirts and blue jeans.

We were spotted as soon as we came
into the woods to hike!

Not all the living things here are hiding.

We see some big white birds.

They are ready to fly up from the marsh.

It will be exciting to watch them fly off.

10

The butterfly is exciting to see.
It has bright, sparkling wings.

The butterfly shuts its wings to hide its spots. Then it hides among the dull leaves.

It doesn't want to become another animal's lunch!

3

Jim tells me to be still.

I look up, down, and sideways to see what he sees.

A handsome snake is sitting in a tree.
The snake looks just like the tree.

Is that a turtle?
It looks just like the grass.
We hardly see it because its spots make it look like the marsh grasses.

Wait, what is that?

It's a green lizard with a long tail.

We wouldn't have spotted it if it hadn't come so close to us.

Now it is racing away.

8

There is a marsh near the woods.

Bugs like the damp marshland, and the bugs like Jim and me.

We don't see the bugs until they bite us!

5

We see a crab moving along the banks
of the marsh.

We didn't see it until it moved, because
it looks like the dirt and sand.

Now it sees us and moves away quickly,
crawling sideways as it goes.

6

Is that a deer or just the sparkling sun
shining through the trees?

Look! There are three handsome deer.

The deer have turned their heads
sideways, spotted us, and run off.

7

TAKE-HOME BOOK
Something New
Use with "The Enormous Turnip."

Answers: 1. granddaughter; 2. seeds; 3. planted; 4. grew; 5. strong;
6. enormous; 7. turnip; 8. hen

Jill and the Giant

by **Alex Vern**
illustrated by Ruth J. Flanigan

Get the Hen

Help Jill get to the top of the plant. Start at number 1. On a sheet of paper, write a word from the turnip to complete the sentence. Keep going until you reach the top. (Turn the page to find the answers.)

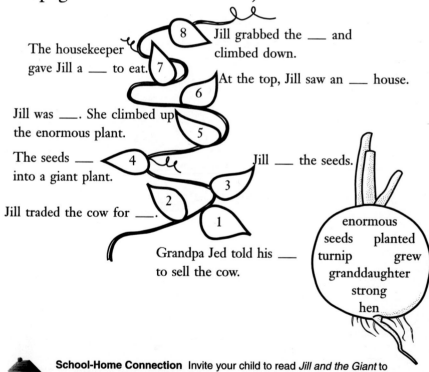

8   Jill grabbed the ___ and climbed down.

The housekeeper gave Jill a ___ to eat.   7

At the top, Jill saw an ___ house.

6

Jill was ___. She climbed up the enormous plant.   5

The seeds ___ into a giant plant.   4

Jill ___ the seeds.

3

Jill traded the cow for ___.   2

1

Grandpa Jed told his ___ to sell the cow.

enormous
seeds   planted
turnip   grew
granddaughter
strong
hen

School-Home Connection Invite your child to read *Jill and the Giant* to you. Then ask your child which parts of the book could be true and which parts could only be make-believe.

Jill gave the hen to Grandpa Jed.

"Thank you, Granddaughter," he said.
"What a smart girl you are!"

Each week, the hen laid a gold egg.
Grandpa Jed, Jill, and Max always had
food. They were happy forever after.

12

A kind man named Jed lived with his
granddaughter, Jill. Max, the cat, lived with
them, too. Jed, Jill, and Max had very little
to eat. Then one day, the food was gone.

"Granddaughter, you must sell the cow,"
said Grandpa Jed.

1

So Jill and Max took the cow to town. On the way, they saw a lady. She was selling some goods by the road.

"I have some wonderful seeds," said the lady. "Plant them and see what they can do."

Max and Jill climbed down the enormous plant. The giant got up and climbed down after them. Jill was smart, and Jill was strong. She cut down the plant with an ax. The giant fell to the ground.

Jill raced away with the hen. The giant raced after her. He was only eight feet away! Max tripped the giant, and the giant fell down.

10

Jill traded the cow for the seeds. Then Jill and Max took the seeds home. Grandpa Jed was surprised.

"How could you do this?" asked Grandpa Jed.

"Now we have no food at all!"

3

Jill and Max went outside and planted the seeds. That night, the seeds grew into a plant. The plant grew and grew until it was enormous.

The giant was full after he ate his turnip. He was soon fast asleep and snoring. Jill grabbed the hen and put it under her coat. The hen clucked, and the giant woke up!

The giant ate a bigger turnip than Jill had eaten. Then he brought out a special hen that laid a shiny gold egg.

"Grandpa Jed told me that my father had a hen like that," Jill said to Max. "That hen must be ours!"

In the morning, Jill and Max saw the enormous plant. It looked very thick and strong. Jill and Max were strong, too. Together they climbed until they reached the top of the plant.

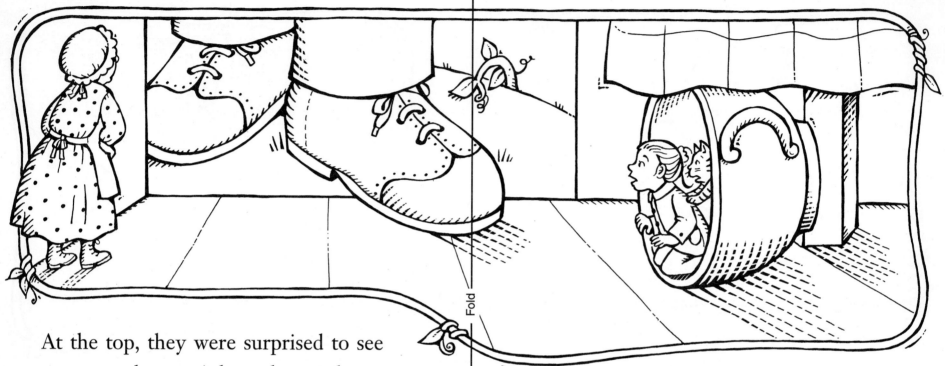

At the top, they were surprised to see an enormous house. A housekeeper let them in. She gave them an enormous turnip to eat.

"An enormous person must live in this enormous house and eat this enormous food," said Jill.

Jill was right. Soon she and Max heard loud footsteps outside the door. Jill hid, and Max hid, too. From their hiding place, they saw a giant come in.

TAKE-HOME BOOK
Something New
Use with "Helping Out."

Fold

by Kathryn Corbett
illustrated by Dave Blanchette

Need Some Help?

Make a poster that tells about a chore you could do to help others. Draw a picture of yourself doing the chore using any tools that you need. Write sentences offering your help with this chore. Share your poster with classmates.

 School-Home Connection Ask your child to read *Help!* to you. Then help your child find the rhyming words in the story. Ask him or her to use them in rhyming sentences.

Fold

Both jobs now seemed so simple.

Everything was done.

When good friends help each other,

Their chores can seem like fun!

12

Raccoon was feeling sad because

His engine wouldn't run.

It wouldn't pull his little train.

Raccoon could not have fun.

1

"I just can't fix this engine.
I don't know why it broke.
It will not sing its chug-chug song
Or make its puffs of smoke."

2

They gathered up the garden tools,
And Rabbit thanked her friend.
"Raccoon, you'll have some ears of corn
Before the summer's end."

11

Raccoon and Rabbit turned the dirt.

They pulled out all the weeds.

They made a scarecrow so the birds

Would not eat up the seeds.

10

Rabbit was upset because

Her garden wouldn't sprout.

The birds were digging up the seeds

And weeds were all about.

3

"I like to grow a garden,
But not to dig or weed.
It's really hard to do the chores
Without the tools I need."

"Thank you, thank you, Rabbit!"
Raccoon said with a cheer.
"Now let's make your garden sprout.
I have the tools right here."

Rabbit sat beside Raccoon
And showed him what to do.
They took apart the engine
And made it run like new.

8

Rabbit left her garden
And went to see Raccoon
She said, "I'll fix your engine.
We'll have it working soon."

5

"Fixing something broken
Is a simple job for me.
I will fix your train set—
You just wait and see!"

6

"I'll bring my fixing tools and work
Right alongside you.
We will fix your engine.
It may just need some glue."

7

TAKE-HOME BOOK
Something New
Use with "Mr. Putter and Tabby Fly the Plane."

Answers:

1. Ladybug eats lunch.
3. Ladybug asks Fly to teach her to fly.
4. Fly gets some leaves.
7. Ladybug gets on Fly's back.
8. Ladybug flies.

Fold

WHY LADYBUGS CAN FLY

by Betsy Franco
illustrated by Bill Ogden

Ladybug's Spots

On a sheet of paper, only write the sentences that tell what happened in the story. Read these sentences to retell the story. (Turn the page to find the answers.)

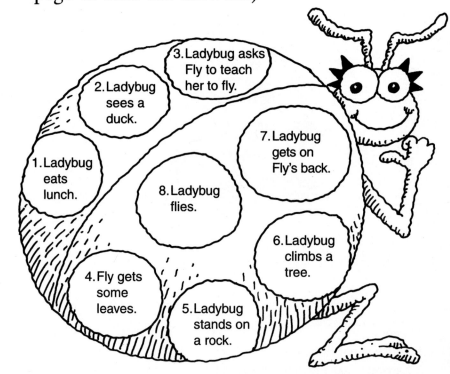

1. Ladybug eats lunch.
2. Ladybug sees a duck.
3. Ladybug asks Fly to teach her to fly.
4. Fly gets some leaves.
5. Ladybug stands on a rock.
6. Ladybug climbs a tree.
7. Ladybug gets on Fly's back.
8. Ladybug flies.

School-Home Connection Invite your child to read *Why Ladybugs Can Fly* to you. Ask whether your child liked the story and why.

But Ladybug let go and started to fall. Then . . . little wings came out from under her shell! Ladybug flapped the little wings. She could fly!

"Look, Fly!" she said. "I have wings! Now I can fly like you!"

And ever since that day, all ladybugs have been able to fly.

12

Fly and Ladybug were best friends. One day they were eating lunch under a web. Three butterflies flew by. The butterflies were pretty. They had pretty colors on their wings.

1

"I've always wanted to fly like the butterflies," said Ladybug to Fly. "You know how to fly. Could you teach me? Please promise that you'll teach me, Fly."

2

"Throw away those leaf wings," Fly said to Ladybug. "Climb up on my back. We can fly together. Hold on tight! Here we go!"

Fly flew up high.

11

Two more butterflies flew by. Fly started to think. Suddenly he had a wonderful idea.

"Butterflies have wings, and I have wings," thought Fly. "I will share my wings with Ladybug."

10

"I promise that I'll try to teach you," said Fly. "It could be hard for you to fly without wings."

At that time, ladybugs did not have wings.

3

Fly said, "How can I teach you to fly? I know! I have an idea. We'll make wings for you from these leaves. Tuck the leaves in your arms, and give them a try!"

4

Fly started to worry. Ladybug was looking sad. She was feeling bad.

"How can I keep my promise to Ladybug? How can I teach her to fly?"

9

"Now jump," said Fly.

"If you jump, your wings will flap.
Then you will fly like the butterflies."

Ladybug jumped from the crane. At
first, she was in the air. Then she fell down
into some leaves.

8

"What do I do?" asked Ladybug.

"I will give you directions," said Fly.

"Flap your wings up and down
like this."

Fly flapped his wings. He flew all
around Ladybug.

5

"Now you try flapping your leaf wings," said Fly.

So Ladybug flapped her wings. She wiggled and jiggled. She hopped and jumped. She groaned and shouted, but her leaf wings would just twitch. They twitched a lot, but they didn't ever flap.

6

"Now what do I do?" asked Ladybug.

"Listen to these directions," said Fly.

"We'll try something new. Do you see those cranes? Get up on one of the cranes."

Ladybug climbed onto a crane.

7

TAKE-HOME BOOK
Something New
Use with "Hedgehog Bakes a Cake."

Answers: 1. sick; 2. cake; 3. Dan; 4. recipe;
5. buttery; 6. batter; 7. funny; 8. Henry;
letters from boxes — iadrbtyh = birthday

Birthday Cookies

by Julie Verne
illustrated by Len Ebert

Fold

What's in the Cookie?

Number a sheet of paper from 1 to 8. Write words from the cookie to complete the sentences. Put a box around the right letter of each. Then make a word from the letters in the boxes. (Turn the page to find the answers.)

Cookie words: sick Henry funny batter cake buttery recipe Dan

1. Papa is ___ ☐ ___ ___.

2. Papa can't make the yellow ___ ☐ ___ ___.

3. ☐ ___ ___ and Jan want to make cookies.

4. They read the simple ☐ ___ ___ ___ ___ ___.

5. They make a ☐ ___ ___ ___ ___ ___ ___ batter.

6. They stir the buttery ___ ___ ☐ ___ ___ ___ .

7. Some cookies had ___ ___ ___ ___ ☐ shapes.

8. ☐ ___ ___ ___ ___ baked the cookies.

School-Home Connection Have your child read *Birthday Cookies* aloud to you. Ask what kind of birthday cake your child might like. Then ask how many candles would be on your child's cake.

Fold

"What beautiful cookies," Mama said.
"There are 10, 20, 30, 40, 41 of them! You
made 40 cookies for 40 happy years! What
a wonderful birthday surprise!"

12

"It's Mama's birthday, and there is no
birthday cake," said Jan.

"Papa always makes the cake," said
Dan. "He uses the same special recipe
for yellow cake every time it's Mama's
birthday."

1

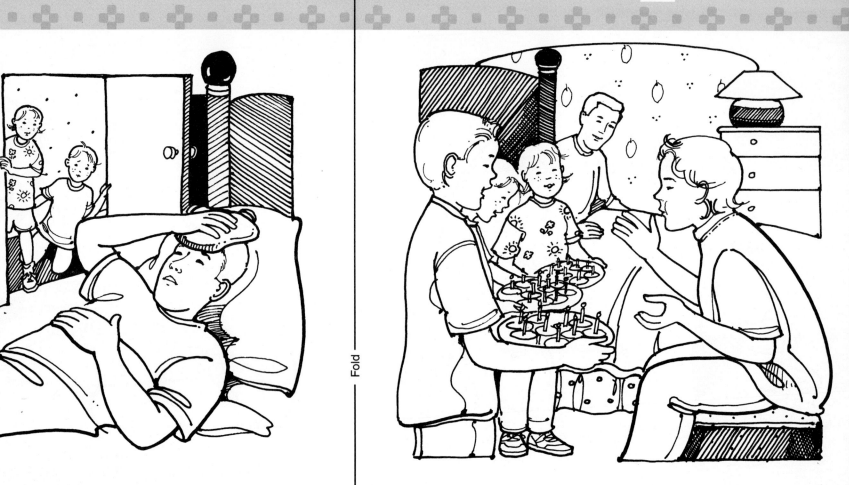

"But Papa is sick in bed," said Jan. "He can't make the yellow cake he always makes for Mama."

"Will Mama's birthday be spoiled?" asked Dan.

2

Papa lit the candles. Then they all called to Mama.

Mama was so surprised! Everyone sang "Happy Birthday."

Then Mama blew out the candles.

11

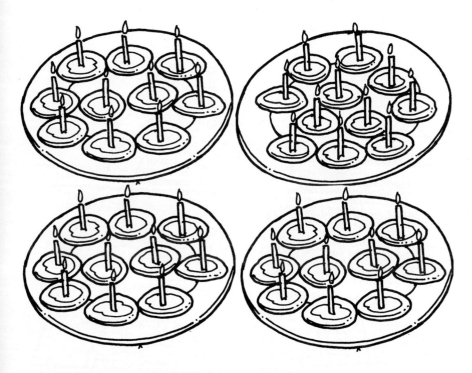

Dan and Jan looked at their cookies. Some of the cookies were round. Others had funny shapes. But there were 41 cookies!

Jan and Dan put a birthday candle on each cookie. Henry helped them take the cookies to Papa's room.

10

"No," said Jan. "We will make something for Mama."

"But how can we make a yellow cake?" asked Dan. "It would be too hard for us to make a cake."

"We will make something else," said Jan.

3

"Maybe we can make birthday cookies for Mama," said Jan. "Henry can help us."

"Okay," said Dan. "Cookies will be quick to make and good to eat. Mama's birthday will not be spoiled!"

"You're right," said Jan. "Let's get started!"

4

"We have 10, 20, 30, 40, 41 cookies," said Jan. "We have 40 cookies and 1 for good luck."

"That's perfect," said Dan. "Mama will be surprised!"

9

Jan and Dan made 31 more enormous birthday cookies.

Then they smeared the baked cookies with frosting.

"Now we have 41 perfect birthday cookies," Dan said.

8

Jan and Dan found a simple recipe.

Then they followed the directions.

They mixed butter and eggs to start the batter.

Then they added flour and stirred.

Soon they had a buttery batter.

5

The buttery batter was perfect.

Jan and Dan smeared butter on a cookie sheet.

Then they made 10 enormous birthday cookies.

Henry put the cookies in to bake.

"Mama is 40 today, so we need to make 40 cookies," said Dan.

"We need to make 41 because we need one for good luck," said Jan.

"That's right," said Dan. "We need 41 cookies."

TAKE-HOME BOOK
Something New
Use with "Lemonade for Sale."

by Daniel Barnes
illustrated by Dave Sullivan

Fold

Meeting Place

Think of another place the club members could meet if they could not rebuild the tree house. Draw a picture of this place. Then write a sentence telling why it would be a good place to meet.

 School-Home Connection Listen as your child reads *The Tree House*. Then ask your child to draw or tell you about a tree house he or she might like to build.

After the storm, all the club members ran to the tree house.

We wondered what it would look like.

Our tree house looked great! We all cheered.

Then we went up to have our meeting. This time we did!

12

All the members of our club were in the tree house.

"Let's have a meeting," I said.

Then I heard the sound of thunder.

I peeked outside.

"It looks as if a big storm is coming!" I announced. "Look at the clouds!"

1

We climbed down from the tree house
and ran home fast.

It's not safe to be in a tree house
in a storm.

We all knew that.

Everyone knows that.

2

We ran to my home and watched
from inside.

We felt very glum again.

What would happen to our new
tree house?

We hoped this tree house was stronger
than the old one.

11

Just before the meeting started, it began
to rain.

Then we heard the sound of thunder
far away.

"Oh, no!" I said. "I think a big storm is
coming. Let's get out of here!"

The next day, we went back to the
tree house.

When we arrived, we looked and
felt glum.

We were glum for a good reason.

Our tree house was not looking
very good!

"The top and the sides of our tree house blew off in the storm," I said.

"We hardly have a tree house left," Tim said. "What are we going to do?"

Something had to be done.

4

We looked at the tree house.
It looked even better than it did before.
We felt proud, and we cheered.
Then we climbed up to have our first meeting in the new tree house.

We all helped rebuild the tree house.
Rosa and Al's mother was a big help.
She's a builder!
It took us two weeks to rebuild. Then
we had our tree house again!

8

"Listen, everyone," I said.
"We all loved our tree house. We
should rebuild it. We can make it even
better than it was before."
The other club members started
to smile.

5

"You two can find some wood," I said to Ted and Bev.

"Let's use the wood from our old fruit stand," they announced.

"We need tools to rebuild our tree house," I said. "Rosa and Al can get some tools, and I will gather the old wood."

6

Ted and Bev arrived back at the tree house with wood from their old fruit stand.

Rosa and Al came back with tools. Their mother came, too.

We were ready to rebuild.

No one was glum anymore!

7

TAKE-HOME BOOK
Something New
Use with "Johnny Appleseed."

Answers: 1. F;   2. T;   3. F;   4. T;   5. F;   6. T;   7. F;   8. F;
9. T;   10. T

On the Wild Frontier

by Betty Verovitz
illustrated by Laurel Aiello

Fold

Frontier Facts

Read each sentence below. Then number a sheet of paper from 1 to 10. Write *T* if the sentence is true. Write *F* if it is false. (Turn the page to find the answers.)

1. Families did not take meat on the trip.
2. The children played tag and other games.
3. There was no way to bake bread on the trip.
4. Families took dried fruits and vegetables on the trip.
5. Families left on their trips in the winter.
6. Wagons sometimes had to be floated across rivers.
7. The trail was flat all the way across the country.
8. People did not take pets on the trip.
9. Before winter, people built houses.
10. In spring, families cleared the land.

School-Home Connection Invite your child to read *On the Wild Frontier* to you. Then discuss the pictures. Ask your child what is happening in each one.

Fold

Why did families travel to the frontier?
They wanted to make new homes. They
wanted to tame the land and to farm.
They wanted to plant orchards.

What are some new frontiers today?
Why might families want to travel there?

12

A long time ago, families traveled to the
frontier. It was a hard trip across wild land.
But one by one, they made up their minds
to go. They wanted to tame some land and
make new homes in the West.

1

Families had to plan their trips to the frontier. They needed horses, cows, and hens to start their new lives on the frontier. They needed wagons in which to carry their food and clothes and tools. They needed oxen to pull their wagons.

2

When spring came, people cleared the land. Then they could plant vegetable gardens and apple orchards. They used seeds from home. The gardens and orchards grew on the frontier lands.

11

Families had to build their homes before the snow came. They needed shelter from the weather. Most people used wood to build their houses. They helped each other to make the work go faster.

10

What did people take to eat? They took a lot of different foods. They needed dried fruits and vegetables. They took flour, rice, eggs, tea, and salt. They took some dried meat, too. They also hunted for meat along the way.

3

Families began their trips in the spring. That was the nicest time of year. It was safer for them to travel west in groups. People helped each other survive dangers. What do you think some of the dangers were?

4

Families stopped in different places. Sometimes when one family stopped to make a home, other families found land nearby. Then these families could help each other. People stopped before winter because it was hard to survive on the trail in winter.

9

Fold

Children had chores to do along
the way. They found fruit, fresh water
to drink, and wood for the fire.
Children also helped bake bread and
watch for danger.

8

People needed to be careful of the wild
animals, which were sometimes nearby.
The land was hard to travel on. There
were muddy rivers for the wagons to float
across. There were mountains to climb.
Also, the weather could be too cold or
too dry.

Fold

There were other things to fear on the way, too. The storms could be very strong. Some people got very sick, and others were bitten by snakes. There wasn't always food to eat. The people could get very hungry.

6

Families also had fun on the trail. Children played tag and other games. The boys and girls liked to play with their pets, which they had brought from home. At night, families sang together by the fire.

7

TAKE-HOME BOOK
Something New
Use with "From Seed to Plant."

Answers: 1. pumpkins;   2. Rex;   3. stream;   4. yard;   5. flowers;
6. seeds

Fold

The Seed Surprise

by Julie Verne
illustrated by Bill Ogden

What's That Word?

Copy numbers 1–6 below on a sheet of paper. Find and write a word from the story to answer each question. Then make a story word from the letters in the boxes. (Turn the page to find the answers.)

1.
What grows on the plant that Sam finds?

— — — — — — — ☐

2.
What is the name of Sam's dog?

— ☐ —

3.
Where does Sam clean the pumpkins?

— — — ☐ — —

4.
Where does Sam find a plant?

— — — ☐

5.
What are the yellow things Sam sees?

— — — — — — ☐

6.

☐ ☐ ☐ ☐ ☐

 School-Home Connection Listen as your child reads *The Seed Surprise* to you. Then discuss the stages of a pumpkin plant from seed to sprout to flower to fruit. Have your child show you the picture in the book for each stage.

Sam cuts some of the pumpkins. His friends cut others. A lot of seeds spill out of the pumpkins! Rex digs in the yard, and many seeds go into the soil.

What do you think will happen next?

12

It is spring. Outside in the yard, Sam sees something green and very little.

"What will this little green sprout grow into?" Sam wonders.

1

Sam wants to protect the growing plant in the middle of the yard. His dog, Rex, likes to dig in the yard! Sam protects the plant with sticks and string.

2

When all the pumpkins ripen, Sam has too many! He calls his friends to come to his yard. They are happy to help Sam with the pumpkins!

11

Winter passes, and spring comes again. Sam sees a lot of green sprouts growing in his yard. This time, he knows what they are. He knows they will grow into pumpkins. Sam protects all the pumpkin plants from Rex.

The plant needs sun, water, and rich soil for good nutrition. If it gets good nutrition, it will grow well.

It is summer now. Sam remembers to water his plant every day. The plant is growing very fast. It seems to be bigger every day.

Sam cuts faces into his pumpkins. When he takes the pumpkins away, many seeds are still on the ground. When Rex digs in the yard, the seeds go into the soil. The soil protects them.

Sam puts the pumpkin into the stream behind his house. He wants to get the rest of the seeds out. Sam watches the pumpkin seeds float off down the stream. He knows they will travel far away to other places.

8

One day, Sam sees beautiful yellow flowers on his plant.

"Stay away, Rex," says Sam. "I don't want you to spoil the beautiful flowers. These flowers will turn into something special. I just know it."

5

Sam is very surprised when the flowers turn into green pumpkins. The pumpkins are small to begin with, but soon they will be enormous. In fall, when each one ripens, Sam can pick them!

6

After each pumpkin ripens, Sam's dad cuts its strong stem. Then he cuts off the top. Sam takes out the seeds. There are so many pumpkin seeds inside!

7

TAKE-HOME BOOK
Something New
Use with "Watermelon Day."

Possible answers: 1. The first time we tried to get food, the people were having relay races. 2. I am Mark. I like to eat chips the best. 3. We ants are happy because people come to the park and leave us food. 4. We ants live in an anthill under an oak tree in Popper Park.

Fold

The Ants and the People

by Mitzie Damon
illustrated by Scott A. Schneidly

Cartoon Fun

On a sheet of paper, copy and complete each ant's sentences. Then make speech balloons around the sentences. Draw the ants who are telling about the story. (Turn the page to find the answers.)

 School-Home Connection Ask your child to read *The Ants and the People* to you. Then choose roles and read the book as a play.

Narrator: The ants have a lot of food in their snug little anthill. They are happy beneath the oak tree.

Fannie: Maybe it's okay to share the park with people after all.

Jake: I wonder when they'll be back.

Abby and Mark: Soon, we hope!

Characters

Narrator	The Ants
Joe	Mark
Joe's mom	Jake
	Fannie
	Abby

Setting

The play takes place in a park. It is afternoon.

Narrator: Fannie and her friends, Mark, Abby, and Jake, live in Popper Park. They like their snug anthill beneath the oak tree.

Fannie: People are always at our park.

Jake: Maybe we should call it People Park!

2

Narrator: The people go off to play again. The ants come back to the wrinkled tablecloth.

Abby: We can gnaw on the hot dogs!

Jake: I want the hot-dog buns!

Mark: I get to eat the chips!

Fannie: They left cake!

Abby: Let's work together to take food home. It will be like a relay race!

11

Narrator: The boy's mother has come to find the boy. She has knelt by him.

Mother: What do you see down here, Joe?

Joe: I see a group of busy ants. What do you think they're doing?

Mother: Maybe they're looking for food. We'll leave some crumbs when we go.

Fannie: Here come more people.

Jake: I can hear their loud footsteps.

Abby: I can feel the ground shake when they walk.

Mark: I hope they don't step on our anthill!

Fannie: I hope they have good things to eat!

Abby: I smell hot dogs! Yum!

Jake: Are there buns? Buns are good!

Mark: Chips are the best! I want chips!

Fannie: Cakes are fun to eat.

Narrator: The ants wait beneath the oak tree for a safe time to go out.

4

Narrator: A boy sees the ants. He has knelt on one knee right next to Abby.

Mark: Watch out, Abby! That boy is a giant! You must run, run, run!

Narrator: The boy just kneels there and watches the ants march away.

9

Fold

Narrator: Just then, the people start to run again. This time there are no relay races. People are running to get cake!

Abby: Oh, no! It's the running feet again! We have to turn back!

Jake: We'll be hungry!

Fannie: But we'll be safe!

Narrator: When they think it's safe, the ants march out. Just then, the people start to run relay races.

Jake: Look at all those big feet!

Abby: We'll be stepped on! Let's go home!

Mark: Then we won't have food!

Fannie: At least we'll be safe!

Fold

Narrator: The hot sun shimmered on the people's picnic. It shimmered on the wrinkled tablecloth and on the food. Seeing the food made the ants hungry.

Abby: Look at those hot dogs!

Jake: Look at those hot-dog buns!

Mark: I see chips!

Fannie: I see cake!

Mark: We'll have a feast!

All the ants: Let's go get some lunch!

Narrator: The ants line up behind Mark. They march out to get some food.

TAKE-HOME BOOK
Something New
Use with "When the Wind Stops."

Answers:

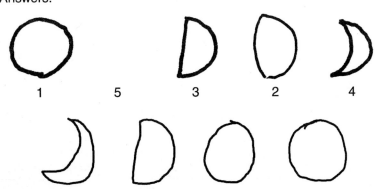

1   5   3   2   4

Dale Lightfoot
and the
Moon

by Betsy Franco
illustrated by Shelley Dieterichs

Fold

Moon Gazing

Here are some of the pictures that Dale painted. Copy them on a sheet of paper. Then number them in the order Dale painted them.

___   ___   ___   ___   ___

Then draw pictures like Dale's to show the moon getting bigger again. (Turn the page to find the answers.)

 School-Home Connection Ask your child to read *Dale Lightfoot and the Moon* to you. Then look for the moon in the sky. Discuss the phase the moon is in.

"You have painted the moon each night," said Grandfather. "You have learned about its pattern. The next time I go to the mountains, you may come with me."

Dale smiled. He was ready!

12

Dale Lightfoot loved his grandfather. His grandfather told him about the stars and the trees. He showed Dale how to hike safely in the mountains.

1

Grandfather showed Dale how to paint, too. Dale learned how to mix different colors from yellow, blue, and red paint. Dale enjoyed learning how to paint the stars and the trees and the mountains.

2

When Dale was painting a glowing, round moon for the third time, Grandfather came back. He joined Dale while Dale was still painting. Dale was happy to have Grandfather home again.

11

Dale's paintings got better as the moon got smaller and then bigger again. He tacked up these paintings under the first set and looked at the pattern.

10

It was autumn. One night Grandfather pointed to the moon and said, "I am going to the mountains. The moon is completely round tonight. When it has been completely round again and then again, I will be back. Paint the moon each night. You will see a pattern."

3

Dale loved the time when the day became a dusky gray. That's when things grew quiet. When the dusky gray turned to black, Dale set up his paints. He looked for the glowing moon in the sky. Then he started to paint.

4

Dale tacked his paintings onto the wall in order. Then he studied them. Dale thought he knew what the moon would look like next. He thought he knew the pattern. "When the moon is completely round again, Grandfather will be back," he said.

9

Then the moon showed again and started to grow. But it was pointed the other way in the sky!

First, the moon was a sliver. Next, it turned into a last-quarter moon. Then it was a round, glowing ball again. This had taken about four weeks.

At first Dale painted outside at night. But soon the autumn nights turned cold. Then Dale painted the moon from his window. From there he could see the sky and the trees and the mountains.

Each night, Dale painted the moon just as he saw it in the sky. The first moon Dale painted was completely round. Nights passed, and Dale saw that the moon was no longer completely round. It was smaller.

The moon became a first-quarter moon and then just a sliver of a moon. One night, Dale could not see the moon at all in the sky. That night, he painted just the dark sky and the bright stars.

TAKE-HOME BOOK
Something New
Use with "What Makes Day and Night."

Fold

A COOL EXPERIMENT

by Daniel Barnes
illustrated by Kathie Kelleher

Night or Day?

Think of something done at night and something done in the daytime. Write your ideas on a sheet of paper. Draw pictures of your nighttime and daytime activities.

night	day
look at stars	sunbathe

 School-Home Connection Listen as your child reads *A Cool Experiment* to you. Then help your child figure out how many hours he or she usually sleeps and how many hours she or he is usually awake.

Fold

Fold

Imagine that you could visit Makiko. Then you would have to get used to her time! Why? That's the way the Earth spins! When one side has day, the other has night!

12

Think about where you live—in the United States. Imagine that you have a friend named Makiko. She lives on the other side of the world in a country called Japan. Can you find Japan on the globe?

1

Fold

If you have a globe and a lamp, you can try an experiment. Put your lamp near the globe. Then turn on the lamp, and turn off all the other lights. The rest of the room should be dark.

2

After a while, Makiko would get used to the different time. She would play all day and sleep at night. When she called home, she would have to think about what time it was there. She would not want to wake anybody up!

11

Makiko might get here in the afternoon, but feel as if it were night. She might want to go to sleep. Then she would not want to sleep at night!

10

Put some clay on the globe to show where you live. Then put some clay on the other side of the globe to show where Makiko lives. Now imagine that the lamp is the sun. The globe is Earth.

3

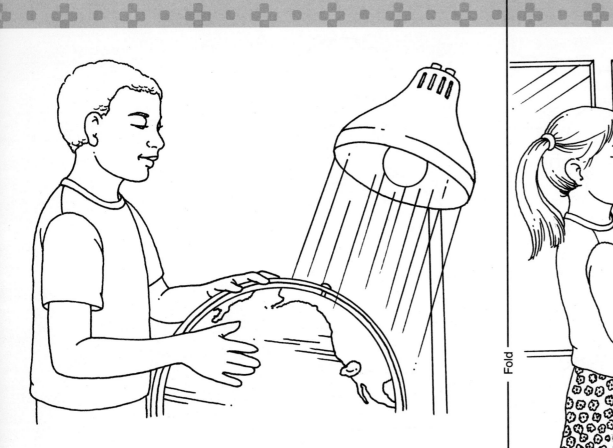

When the globe spins, its motion is like the motion of Earth as it spins. Spin the globe so that the United States is turned toward the light. It is daytime for you. There is no light where Makiko lives. It is nighttime for her.

4

What would happen if Makiko came to visit you for a month? For the first few days, Makiko might feel mixed up about the time. Why do you think she might be mixed up?

9

If you put your photograph and Makiko's next to each other, you would see something odd. "Wow!" you might say. "We took these pictures at the same time, but in my picture it's daytime. In Makiko's, it's night!"

8

Spin the globe so that Makiko's home is turned toward the light. Now it is daytime for her. There is no light where you live. It is nighttime for you.

5

Now think about another experiment. Imagine that you call Makiko on the phone. Then you both go outside right after the phone call. You ask someone to take two photographs of you. Makiko asks someone to take two photographs of her.

6

Imagine that you keep one photograph of yourself and mail the other photograph to Makiko. Makiko mails you one of her photographs, too.

When you get her picture, what do you think you will see?

7

TAKE-HOME BOOK
Just In Time
Use with "The Day Jimmy's Boa Ate the Wash."

Answers: 1. wake up   2. milk cow   3. get eggs   4. feed pigs
5. eat lunch   6. pick fruits and vegetables   7. ride horse, swim,
play   8. help at farm stand   9. go to bed

Fold

Never Bored on the Farm

by Alex Vern
illustrated by Marion Eldridge

A Day on the Farm

Number a sheet of paper from 1 to 9.
Write the things listed on the haystack in
the order in which the boy does them in
the story. (Turn the page to find the
answers.)

milk cow
feed pigs
go to bed
get eggs
wake up
ride horse, swim, play
eat lunch
pick fruits and vegetables
help at farm stand

 School-Home Connection Ask your child to read *Never Bored on the Farm* to you. Then ask which farm job your child might like to do.

Is it boring on my farm? Some people might think so, but I am never, ever bored on my farm! Would you like to spend a day on the farm with me?

It's never boring on a farm. I know because I live on a farm. I suppose I should tell you that I have to wake up early. I suppose I should say that I get tired sometimes, but I would never tell you that life is boring here on my farm!

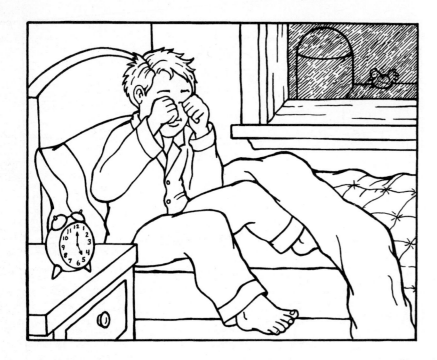

Every morning, I get up before the sun rises. I don't wait for the rooster to say "Cock-a-doodle-do." I get up at five o'clock! I suppose I could wait for the sun to rise. I suppose I could wait for the rooster to crow, but that wouldn't make sense. I'd never get my chores done!

2

Before I know it, it's time to get up. My alarm clock is ringing. It's five o'clock. Off I go to milk the cow again!

11

Each night, I go to bed tired but happy.
I fall asleep right away. I'm always tired
after a long day of work and play.

First I go to the cow barn. I get my
milking pail and stool. Then I milk a cow.
My dad showed me how last year. He
told me that if I ducked, I could see what
I was doing. That made sense to me! So I
ducked then, and I duck now!

10

3

Fold

After I milk the cow, I go to the chicken coop. That's where the hens live. I scoop up all the eggs and put them in my basket. I suppose I could wait for the hens to give me the eggs, but that wouldn't make sense. I'd be waiting all day. We'd have no eggs to eat!

4

Sometimes I go to bed before sunset. I stop before the sun does! I suppose I could stay up late, but that wouldn't make sense. How would I get up the next morning?

9

Sometimes I help out at our farm stand. We sell fruits and vegetables. I suppose we don't have to have a farm stand. What would we do with all the food we don't eat?

It's my job to feed the pigs, too. They live in the pigsty. The pigs are always loud and muddy. Sometimes they fight over the food. What a mess everything is then! Sometimes I'm a mess, too!

My family eats the food that we grow.
We have eggs and toast in the morning.
Then we eat our big meal at noon. We
have meat, milk from the cows, sweet fruits
from the orchards, and vegetables from the
garden. I suppose we could buy our food,
but that wouldn't make sense when we can
grow our own!

After lunch, I pick fruits from the
orchard and vegetables from the garden. I
suppose I could take a nap, but there's too
much I want to do! I like to ride my horse
or swim in the pond or play hide-and-seek.
There are a lot of places to hide on a farm.

TAKE-HOME BOOK
Just in Time
Use with "How I Spent My Summer Vacation."

Answers: 1. T   2. F   3. T   4. T   5. T   6. F   7. T   8. T

Sitting Around the Campfire

by Dattie Makem
illustrated by George Ulrich

Cattle Facts

Read the sentence in each of the cattle shapes. Then number a sheet of paper from 1 to 8. Write *T* if the sentence is true. Write *F* if the sentence is false. (Turn the page to find the answers.)

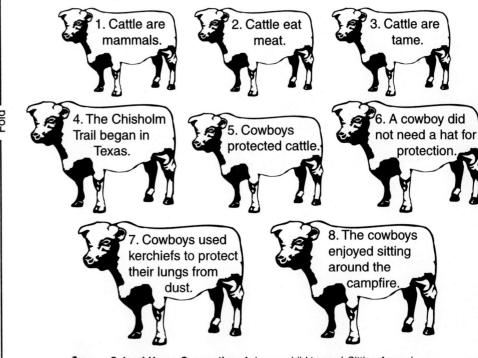

1. Cattle are mammals.

2. Cattle eat meat.

3. Cattle are tame.

4. The Chisholm Trail began in Texas.

5. Cowboys protected cattle.

6. A cowboy did not need a hat for protection.

7. Cowboys used kerchiefs to protect their lungs from dust.

8. The cowboys enjoyed sitting around the campfire.

School-Home Connection Ask your child to read *Sitting Around the Campfire* to you. Ask what your child would want to do if he or she were sitting around a campfire.

It was time to go home, but the cowboys would never forget their vacation. They would always remember sitting around the campfire and talking about cattle, cowboys, and the plains.

12

Some cowboys went on a camping vacation in Kansas. Every night, they sat around the campfire. They shared information about life on the plains in the old West.

1

Bart told about cattle. "Cows and bulls are cattle, and cattle are mammals," he said. "Cattle eat plants like grass. That's why they graze on the plains."

2

"I would be a cowgirl with good manners," the girl said. "I would say *please* and *thank you* to my horse and the cattle. Manners are important!"

11

On the last night, a girl came up to the cowboys. "I want to be a cowgirl," she said. "I would be like a matador. I would hold up a red cloth and make the cattle run! I would be the little matador!"

10

"Did you know that cattle have four parts to their stomachs?" Bart asked. "They have hoofs and horns, too. People first tamed cattle 8,500 years ago!"

3

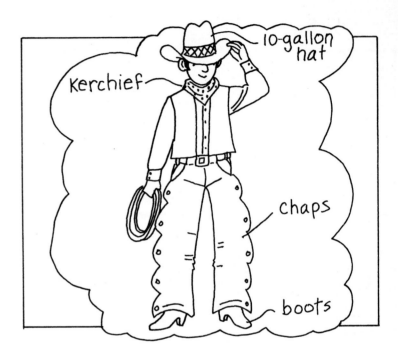

Al took a turn the next night. "Relax around the fire," he said. "I will tell you more about cattle. In the 1800s, cowboys went on cattle drives."

"A cowboy wore special clothes to protect him," Frank said. "His ten-gallon hat protected him from the sun. His kerchief protected his lungs from the dust. His chaps protected his legs from thorns. His boots protected his feet from snakes."

On the fourth night, Frank spoke. "In the old West," he said, "cowboys were hired to protect cattle. Sometimes cattle ran away or were stolen. Then the cowboys captured the cattle and brought them back."

8

"Have you heard of the Chisholm Trail?" Al asked. "It started in Texas. Cowboys took the cattle in a northern direction. The trail ended in Kansas. From there, the cattle were shipped east by train."

5

On the third night, Joe spoke. "Sit back. Relax. Use your imagination," he said. "Imagine that we're all cowboys in 1870. We're on a cattle drive."

"We're riding along on our horses," Joe said. "I see that one cow has wandered away from the rest. I ride after it and swing my rope. I capture the cow!"

Bart laughed. "We would need a good imagination to believe that!" he said.

TAKE-HOME BOOK
Just in Time
Use with "Dear Mr. Blueberry."

Fold

The World Under the Water

by Ted Jamison
illustrated by Eulala Conner

Go Fish

Choose one fish the boy in the story saw while snorkeling. On a sheet of paper, draw and color the fish. Write a fact about the fish under your drawing. You may look for information in an encyclopedia or a book about fish.

A butterfly fish has a long nose!

 School-Home Connection Listen as your child reads *The World Under the Water* to you. Ask your child what else people might see under the water.

Fold

That was the very first time I went snorkeling. Now that I'm older, I snorkel a lot. I never get tired of seeing the world under the water. It is a beautiful and enormous world to see.

12

Have you ever seen fish in the ocean up close? I have, and I'd like to tell you about the first time I did.

I live in Hawaii, a state in the United States. The island I live on is beautiful. The sky is blue. The water is warm.

1

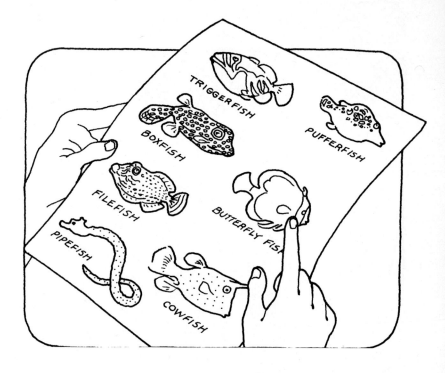

When I was eight, my family and I went snorkeling for the first time. Snorkeling is swimming to look at fish. We had to rent masks with special tubes. The tubes stayed above the water. That's how we could breathe. We rented fins for our feet, too.

We swam back to the beach and looked up information about the fish. We learned the names of all the kinds we had seen. We had seen butterfly fish, pipefish, boxfish, cowfish, filefish, and pufferfish. I think the butterfly fish were the best!

I fed some peas to the fish. I could see the details in their markings. What beautiful fish lived under the water! I wanted to see more and more. Dad had to forcibly make me turn back! I had to forcibly make myself turn back!

The man at the store gave us a lot of good information. We got some maps, and the man showed us where the best beaches were. Then he gave us details about some of the fish we might see. He gave me some peas, too. "You can feed peas to the fish," he told me.

"Don't go into the water alone," the
man told us. "Oceans are very beautiful,
but they are not tame. It's not safe to swim
in any of the oceans alone."

"Snorkeling is a lot of fun," he said
with a smile. "It won't disappoint you."

4

Then I saw more schools of fish. I saw
a whole world of fish under the water.
What I saw didn't disappoint me. The
ocean life was beautiful.

9

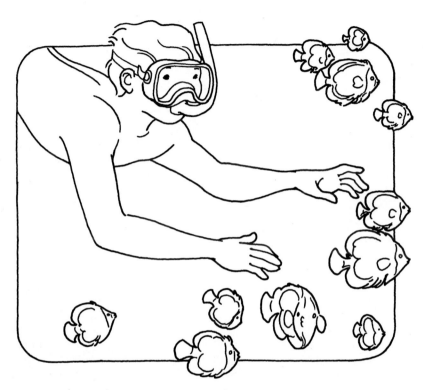

Suddenly I saw a school of yellow-striped fish. Were they butterfly fish? Whatever they were, they were beautiful as they glided by. I wished that I could stroke them. What would their skin feel like? I knew not to stroke the fish.

8

We drove to a small, rocky beach where the water was blue-green. We slipped our fins onto our feet. We put on our masks, too. I thought we looked funny. "We'll scare the fish away," I said.

5

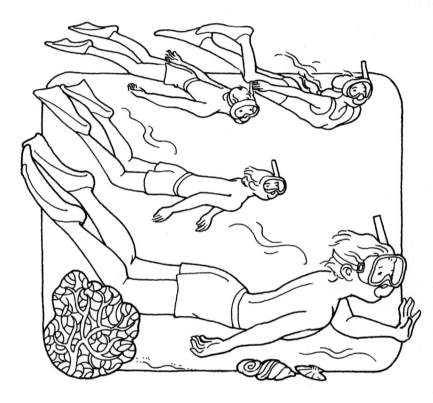

Then my dad said, "We must stay together. Never, ever swim away alone. If we see fish, remember what they look like. If you remember the details, we can look up what kind they are later."

Then we all headed for the ocean. It was hard to walk over the rocks in fins. It was not hard to swim with fins on. The fins made swimming simple. Now that I was swimming, I began to look for fish.

TAKE-HOME BOOK
Just in Time
Use with "It's Probably Good Dinosaurs Are Extinct."

Answers: 1. T   2. F   3. F   4. T   5. T   6. T   7. F   8. T

One of My Bears

by Betsy Franco
illustrated by Jackie Snider

Story Facts

Number a sheet of paper, from 1 to 8. Then read each sentence in the paw prints below. Write *T* if the sentence is true. Write *F* if it is false. (Turn the page to find the answers.)

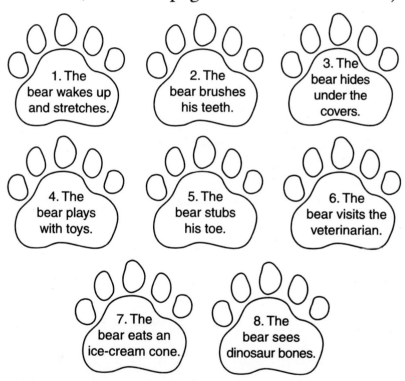

1. The bear wakes up and stretches.

2. The bear brushes his teeth.

3. The bear hides under the covers.

4. The bear plays with toys.

5. The bear stubs his toe.

6. The bear visits the veterinarian.

7. The bear eats an ice-cream cone.

8. The bear sees dinosaur bones.

 School-Home Connection Invite your child to read *One of My Bears* to you. Then ask which things in the story could have really happened and which were make-believe.

But then the bones start moving!
"Bear, save me! Help!" I scream.
I sit right up in bed and find
It's all been just a dream!

12

Is that my Bear that's stretching?
I can't believe my eyes!
But then I hear him say to me,
"Hello, my friend. Surprise!"

1

I tell myself, "Have courage!"
When Bear jumps out of bed.
For now my little furry toy
Is taller than my head!

2

The dinosaur we see is huge!
It's standing by a cave.
"It's only bones," I say to Bear.
He isn't very brave.

"Here we are," I say to Bear.

I open the big door.

"Come on inside with me," I say.

"You'll see your dinosaur."

10

"Bear, wait for me!" How fast he roams!

He's off and out my door.

"Halt! Halt! I can't keep up with you!"

But Bear wants to explore.

3

Downstairs I find him by my shelves.

He's playing with my toys.

"I'll play with you," I offer. "Tell me

What a bear enjoys."

4

The veterinarian is kind.

She looks at Bear's red toe.

She wraps it up and gives him a hug.

Then off again we go!

9

"Have courage, Bear! Just lean on me,"
I say. "I'll help you hop.
We'll visit the veterinarian
Next door to the pet shop."

8

"I want to find a dinosaur,"
He tells me with a smile.
I tell him I'm afraid they've been
Extinct for quite a while.

5

When Bear looks at me sadly,
I tell him, "Don't feel blue.
Dinosaurs may be extinct,
But I'll find one for you."

6

I grab his paw, and off we roam
Until poor Bear yells, "Ow!
A stone was under all these leaves!
I've stubbed my toe! Oh, wow!"

7

TAKE-HOME BOOK
Just in Time
Use with "Cool Ali."

Answers: Pictures will be of Meg doing the following:

playing a game

reading a book

playing hide-and-seek

playing an acting game

painting a picture

It's Raining

by Dana Catharine
illustrated by Marilyn Mets

Picture This!

Meg did five rainy-day activities with Mike. On a sheet of paper, draw a picture of Meg doing each thing. Label each picture. Then circle the activity that Mike enjoyed. (Turn the page to find the answers.)

 School-Home Connection Listen as your child reads *It's Raining* to you. Then ask your child which activity from the story he or she would like best to do on a rainy day. Try that activity with your child!

Fold

Meg and Mike had fun painting outside pictures. They didn't notice when the rain stopped. They didn't notice when the haze lifted outside. They painted and painted until the pale sunlight began to shine. Then they ran out to play!

12

Meg stared out the window. Mike did, too. It was hard to see through the rainy haze. "We'll have to play inside," Meg said.

1

"Let's play this game," Meg said. "We can still have fun."

2

This time Mike didn't fuss. He admired Meg's picture. He admired it so much that he began to paint a picture, too.

11

"Let's imagine that we are outside!" said
Meg. "Think of something fun." She
painted a picture of Mike riding his bike
outside in the pale sunlight.

Mike didn't like the game. He wanted
to play outside. He fussed about it so much
that Meg put away the game.

"Let's read this book," Meg said. "It's a good one."

4

No one mimicked Meg. Mike didn't want to play that game. He wanted to play outside. He fussed about it so much that Meg stopped being a tiger.

9

"Let's play an acting game," said Meg. "Do what I do." Meg mimicked a tiger.

8

Mike didn't care about the book. He wanted to play outside. He fussed about it so much that Meg put the book away.

5

"Let's play hide-and-seek," said Meg.
"That will be fun." Meg hid behind
a chair.

6

Mike just sat on the stairs. He wanted
to play outside. He fussed about it so much
that Meg came out from behind the chair.

7

TAKE-HOME BOOK
Just in Time
Use with "The Park Bench."

Possible answers: Mom (picking cherries); Dad (with a cherry pie); Grandpa (resting or reading in a chair underneath); Kimmy (reading on a low branch); Betty (swinging from a swing on a branch); Danny (climbing on branches); birds in their nests; squirrels playing chase

The Old Cherry Tree

by Mitzie Damon
illustrated by Franklin Ayers

Fold

Who's at the Cherry Tree?

Draw a large cherry tree in the middle of a sheet of paper. Draw all the people and animals from the story by the cherry tree. Show what each one likes to do with the tree. Then label your pictures. Tell who each person or animal is. (Turn the page to find the answers.)

 School-Home Connection Have your child read *The Old Cherry Tree* to you. Then ask him or her to name other kinds of fruit trees.

No one knows how old I am or who planted me, but I'm the oldest, largest cherry tree in sight. People and animals like me for all kinds of reasons. Do you think you would like a tree like me?

I am a cherry tree. I have been around a long time. No one has ever agreed on how old I am. No one knows who planted me. I'm the oldest, largest cherry tree in sight. I must have been planted many, many years ago.

The people who live in the house nearby seem to like me. The animals in the yard like me, too. The people and the animals like me for completely different reasons. What do you think some of those reasons are?

I almost forgot Danny. I think he likes me even more than the rest of his family does. Sometimes Danny climbs all around on my branches. On those days he is as lively as the squirrels! On other days, Danny is as still as Kimmy. He likes to eat cherries as he reads.

Fold

Grandpa comes back at noon to rest. He gets drowsy in the sun. He is so drowsy that he falls asleep. He naps in the gentle breeze. Sometimes the wind blows a few leaves onto Grandpa while he sleeps.

10

The morning mist clears as the sun comes up. Grandpa and his friends sit underneath me. They talk in my shade. Their shoes get wet from the mist on the grass.

3

Of course the birds are up by then and looking for food. They bring it to their nests, which are hidden in my branches. I help the birds by giving them places to build their nests. Up high they are safe from cats and dogs. I like to hear the birds sing.

Betty likes to swing. She goes back and forth, back and forth. Her feet reach for my leaves as she goes up. My branch is very thick and strong. That's why it doesn't hurt me when she swings.

The squirrels are very lively. They race up and down my branches. They chatter all the time as they chase each other. Sometimes they bring nuts up with them. The shells drop down below me. Woof, the dog, likes to chase the squirrels. It's a good thing that he can't climb me!

8

Each morning, Mom comes out to pick fresh cherries. She likes to pick them before they drop to the ground. When she has gathered a lot of cherries, she takes them inside. What do you think Mom and her family do with my cherries?

5

Fold

Dad enjoys making cherry pies from the cherries Mama gathers. Sometimes the family invites friends for a picnic. Everyone laughs and plays and eats cherry pie underneath my branches.

Kimmy likes to climb my branches. She has agreed to be gentle with me. Sometimes Kimmy brings a book with her. Then she perches on a branch and reads quietly. She is as still as the birds that rest in their nests.

TAKE-HOME BOOK
Just in Time
Use with "The Pine Park Mystery."

Answers: 1. crow;   2. robin;   3. woodpecker;   4. pigeon;
5. bald eagle;   6. song sparrow;   7. hummingbird;   8. owl

Fold

All About Birds

by James McGuire
illustrated by Rosiland Solomon

Fold

Riddle Time

Number a sheet of paper from 1 to 8.
Write a bird's name to answer each riddle.
(Turn the page to find the answers.)

1. I am big, smart, and
   black.
   I am a

   _____.

2. I can be a sign of
   spring.
   I am a

   _____.

3. I knock on trees.
   I am a

   _____.

4. I live in the city.
   I have a small head
   and a short neck.
   I am a

   _____.

5. I live near water and
   eat fish.
   I am a

   _____.

6. I may sing 300 times
   in an hour.
   I am a

   _____.

7. I am very small.
   I may be only two
   inches long.
   I am a

   _____.

8. I am a night bird that
   eats mice.
   I am an

   _____.

 School-Home Connection Ask your child to read *All About Birds* to you. Then have your child make up new riddles about the birds. Guess the birds.

Birds of many colors and sizes are found all over the world. On a typical day, look up in the sky. What kinds of birds do you see?

12

Look up in the sky. On a typical day, what objects might you see? Maybe you would see an airplane flying over. Or you might see a kite. What other objects might you see?

1

What animals might you see in the sky on a typical day? Insects, bats, and even squirrels can fly. In the daytime, you might see birds. Birds of many colors and sizes are found all over the world.

North American crows are big, smart, black birds. Crows can be pests when they eat people's gardens. That's what caused people to make scarecrows. Does it look as if the scarecrow is scaring away the crows?

Fold

Song sparrows sing a lot. They may sing 300 times in an hour! Do you think they sing the same song all 300 times? Many song sparrows build their nests on the ground. This sparrow is rebuilding its nest with grasses and roots.

Do you live in the northeastern United States? Robins arriving there in March are a sign of spring. In the southeastern United States, you might see robins in winter. Robins spend winters in the south and summers in the north.

Fold

Bald eagles live near water. They almost always eat fish. But unlike other sea eagles, bald eagles are not good fishers. Most of the time, they eat dead or sick fish. Sometimes they steal fish that other birds catch.

4

Did you hear that hum? It is not caused by a bee. It is the sound of a hummingbird's wings. Hummingbirds are small. The smallest hummingbird is only about two inches long. Is it smaller than the clasp on a watch?

9

What has caused this owl to be awake at night? Do you think it is confused? It is not confused. Owls are night birds. They sleep in the daytime and are awake at night. Their good eyesight helps them find mice to eat. This owl has cornered a mouse.

Do you ever hear a noise that sounds like a knock on a tree? If you look, you might see a woodpecker. A woodpecker uses its bill to make holes in a tree. Then it removes and eats the insects it finds.

Do you live in a city? Then you might see pigeons. A pigeon is a bird with a small head, a short neck, and short legs. Pigeons eat seeds, nuts, and insects.

One pigeon has cornered an insect. One pigeon is eating a peanut. Do you think it removes the shell first? Another pigeon finds a small, shiny clasp from someone's watch. It looks confused. "What is this?" it seems to wonder.

TAKE-HOME BOOK
Just in Time
Use with "Good-bye, Curtis."

Fold

In Eight More Years

by Julie Verne
illustrated by Anne Kennedy

What's in the Mail?

On a sheet of paper, draw five envelopes like the ones below. (Draw them big enough so you can write a sentence in each.) In each envelope, write something you learned about Beth's job.

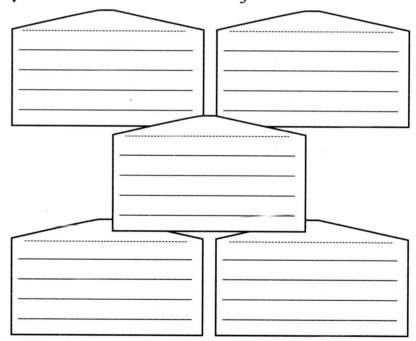

 School-Home Connection Invite your child to read *In Eight More Years* to you. Then look at an addressed envelope you have at home. Discuss the stamp, the postmark, the code along the bottom of the envelope, and the addresses.

In eight more years, I might be a clerk at an ice-cream store. But when I am really grown up, maybe I'll be a mail carrier— just like my sister!

12

Fold

In eight years, I want to be a clerk at an ice-cream store. My sister, Beth, was an ice-cream clerk once. She liked selling ice-cream cones to people. It was her first real job.

1

Fold

One time the store put up a photograph of Beth. It was to honor her for being good at her job. The photo had the words *Clerk of the Week* on it. It was a big honor for Beth. She was very proud.

2

Have you seen something odd about some mail trucks? In cars, the steering wheel is on the left side. In mail trucks, it's on the right side. That way, mail carriers don't have to walk in the street when they get out. They can also put mail in roadside boxes without getting out at all!

11

There is another part to Beth's job. She also picks up letters and packages from mailboxes on the street. There can be a lot of mail inside those big boxes! When Beth opens the box, the mail will pour right out.

10

Now that Beth is grown up, she has a different job. She is a mail carrier. Beth liked being an ice-cream clerk, but she likes this job better. She likes taking the mail to the people on her route.

3

Beth has a lot to do in her job. There are 369 houses on her route. That means she carries the mail for 369 addresses! Beth sorts the mail for her route every morning. Then when she goes on her route, the mail is in order. Beth does not want to mix up people's mail!

4

Beth's job is easier to do in some kinds of weather than in others. When rain pours down, Beth has to wear special rain clothes. Mail carriers must do their routes in all kinds of weather. The mail must always go through.

9

At some times of the year, there is even more mail to deliver. People send a lot of mail around holidays and special days, like Valentine's Day. At these times, Beth has extra mail to carry!

8

Beth has to load the mail into her truck in big trays. Those trays aren't light. Beth says you need to have strong arms to be a mail carrier. Each tray can weigh as much as thirty-five pounds!

5

Beth says that mail carriers need strong legs, too. They have to walk a lot on their routes. Beth walks about seven miles a day to get to all those addresses.

6

Dogs can be a danger to Beth when she is on her route. Some dogs like Beth, but others bark or growl. Some dogs have even tried to bite her. Beth always has to be on the lookout for dogs. She has a special spray to keep growling dogs away from her.

7

TAKE-HOME BOOK
Just in Time
Use with "Max Found Two Sticks."

Answers: 1. junk; 2. cans, tub; 3. spoons; 4. banjo; 5. hose;
6. created; 7. rhythm; 8. conductor; 9. band

Fold

Junk Band

by Jesse Levine
illustrated by Kate Flanagan

Band Time

Number a sheet of paper from 1 to 9.
Write a word from the story to complete
each sentence. Draw boxes around the
letters shown. Then make a word from the
letters in the boxes. (Turn the page to find
the answers.)

1. The friends made a __ __ __ __ band.

2. They used __ __ __ __ and a wash __ __ ☐ .

3. They hit pots and pans with __ __ __ __ __ __ .

4. They made a __ ☐ __ __ __ with a box and rubber bands.

5. They made a horn from a __ __ __ __ .

6. The band played songs that they had __ __ __ __ __ __ ☐ .

7. Their songs had good __ __ __ __ __ __ and good tunes.

8. The train __ __ ☐ __ __ __ __ __ __ liked the band.

9. __ __ __ __

 School-Home Connection Have your child read *Junk Band* to you.
Then make rhythms together by clapping your hands in different beats
and patterns.

Our group had created a great band out of nothing but junk. After our show, other groups of friends wanted to form junk bands, too. We showed them how. Now they're good, we're proud, and we're all having fun!

12

Here's how my group of friends created a junk band. Why do I call it a junk band? We made almost everything from junk!

1

First we made some drums. We used tubs, cans, and a big washtub. Then we grabbed our sticks and imitated rhythms we had heard other bands play. That's how we learned to play rhythm on our drums.

2

We played a lot of songs at our show. When we were through, everyone clapped. We were startled. Did everyone really think we were good? We felt very happy and very proud.

11

Mr. Marks, the train conductor, had given us an idea. We would plan a show for our friends and families. We would ask Mrs. Dix and Mr. Marks to come to hear us, too.

10

Then we got some old pots and pans. We found all sorts of other things that no one wanted, too. We hung our junk from a rope and hit it with spoons. What great sounds we got! Now we could play both rhythms and tunes.

3

We played our music, but something was missing. We got a box and rubber bands and used them to make a banjo. Then we imitated banjo sounds we had heard.

We made a flute from a bottle. Now we were getting a lot of sounds. Our band sounded good!

4

"Your band is getting good," Mr. Marks said. "It's loud, but it's good. I like lively music."

That made us feel very proud. Mr. Marks watched us for a little while. Then he went back inside to sleep.

9

Fold

One day Mr. Marks appeared at his door. Mr. Marks is a train conductor at night. He sleeps in the daytime. We thought he would tell us we were too loud for him to sleep. But he startled us. He began to move to our music!

8

Matt and Jean appeared from around the corner. "Your music startled us," Matt said. "May we play, too?"

Matt made a horn from a garden hose. Jean made a kazoo from a cardboard tube. Matt and Jean played a lot of tunes.

5

All of us wanted our band to sound good. So we chose days and times to get together. We chose songs to play, too.

We played songs we had heard, and we created our own songs, too. Our songs had rhythm. Our songs had good tunes. And our songs were loud!

6

We were too loud for our neighbor, Mrs. Dix. When we played, she closed her doors and windows. But we were lucky. She never asked us to stop playing. She must have remembered being a kid herself!

7

TAKE-HOME BOOK
Just in Time
Use with "Anthony Reynoso: Born to Rope."

Answers:

5	Pepe sees a cat he knows.
2	A man at the market gives Pepe scraps of meat and fish.
4	Pepe walks to a ranch.
6	Pepe finds the girl and his home.
1	At the market, Pepe runs after some mice and gets lost.
3	Pepe watches an exhibition of dancing.

Fold

LOST!

by Maria Bates
illustrated by C. Shana Greger

Pepe's Path

Show what happened in *Lost!*. Copy each sentence and blank below on a sheet of paper. Write 1, 2, 3, 4, 5, and 6 to put the sentences in story order. (Turn the page to find the answers.)

_____ Pepe sees a cat he knows.
_____ A man at the market gives Pepe scraps of meat and fish.
_____ Pepe walks to a ranch.
_____ Pepe finds the girl and his home.
_____ At the market, Pepe runs after some mice and gets lost.
_____ Pepe watches an exhibition of dancing.

 School-Home Connection Invite your child to read *Lost!* to you. Ask whether your child thinks Pepe will sneak away again.

Fold

The girl brushed Pepe's dirty coat.
Soon he was clean again. Pepe had been
brave and smart and strong. He had
made it home!

12

The little cat, Pepe, was very unhappy.
He had sneaked into the car so he could go
with the girl. At the market he had run
after some mice. Now he was lost.

1

Pepe looked everywhere for the girl. He ran up and down and here and there. He couldn't find the girl anywhere. Where was he? Was he thousands of miles from home?

"I'm not really thousands of miles from home," he thought. "I'll find my way home."

2

The girl looked up and saw Pepe. "Where have you been? I've been looking for you everywhere. I'm so glad you're back!"

The girl gave the little cat an enormous hug. Then she rubbed his chin just the way he liked.

11

Pepe began sniffing the ground and the air. He would sniff his way home! Finally he saw the family's landscape business. There was the girl! She was playing in the yard.

10

Pepe walked through the large market. He saw many fruits and vegetables and meats. Pepe was hungry. He was happy when a man gave him scraps of meat and fish. They tasted good to a hungry cat!

3

At the end of the market, Pepe saw an exhibition of dancing. Ladies in bright dresses were turning around and around. The exhibition was fun to watch. There were many people watching and taking photographs. Pepe had to be careful so he wouldn't be stepped on!

4

Pepe came to another town. He saw the street signs. He wished he could read so he would know where he was. Then, when Pepe turned the corner, he saw a cat he knew. "I must be almost home!" he thought.

9

Pepe walked by a place to eat. A kind lady gave him some water and some scraps of food. He felt much stronger after a good meal. Now Pepe didn't feel so unhappy. He felt as if he would make it home.

8

The girl's family was in the landscape business. So Pepe knew about landscape. The landscape near the market was very flat. The landscape near his home was hilly. So Pepe set off toward the hills.

5

After a while, Pepe came to a ranch. There were a lot of brown horses on the ranch. There were a few dappled horses, too. Pepe stopped to lap up some milk from a pail near the barn. The dappled horses seemed to laugh at him. Pepe just groomed himself and went on.

6

Soon Pepe came to a town. People were everywhere, playing music and singing. There were a lot of dogs, too. This was not a good place for a cat! So Pepe went on.

7

TAKE-HOME BOOK
Just in Time
Use with "Montigue on the High Seas."

Answers: 1. winds;   2. coast;   3. Weather;   4. protect;   5. looming

Fold

by Elizabeth Field
illustrated by Lane Yerkes

Launch Your Boats

On a sheet of paper, write the numbers 1–5.
Beside each number, write the word from
the story that completes that sentence.
(Turn the page to find the answers.)

1. The _____ in a hurricane can blow at 100 miles per hour.

2. Hurricanes are strongest over the _____.

3. _____ forecasters track the storm.

4. People want to _____ their boats.

5. Tony and Tina saw dark clouds _____ over the horizon.

School-Home Connection Listen as your child reads *Hurricane!* to you. Then discuss with your child the kinds of storms your area receives.

Fold

The clouds on the horizon were soon looming overhead. The hurricane had arrived. Tony and Tina knew that they would be safe inside their cozy home.

12

Tony and Tina were playing a game. Mom and Dad were watching the news. The weather forecasters were talking about a hurricane.

1

"What is a hurricane?" Tina asked Tony.

"It's a huge, windy rainstorm," Tony told her. "The winds in a hurricane are very strong. They can blow at more than 100 miles per hour!"

2

Tony and Tina saw dark clouds looming on the horizon. They realized that the forecaster had been right.

"We're lucky we don't live on the coast," said Tony. "The hurricane won't be as strong here."

11

"Is the hurricane coming here?" Tina asked Tony. They both ran to the window and looked outside.

10

"Hurricanes begin over the ocean," said Tony. "Sometimes they travel toward land. If they reach land, they're strongest over the coast. Hurricanes cause the most damage there."

3

"How do people know when there will be a hurricane?" asked Tina.

"Weather forecasters can track the storms. They tell people where the hurricane might go. Then people can get ready for the storm."

4

Just then Tony and Tina realized that the weather forecasters were still talking about the hurricane. One forecaster said the storm was headed their way!

9

"Sometimes people must leave their homes before a hurricane comes," said Tony. "They want to stay in their cozy homes, but their homes might not stay cozy. Water could come in from the ocean!"

8

"How do people get ready?" asked Tina. "One thing they do is protect their boats," Tony said. "People don't want their boats to drift out to sea."

"What would happen if a fleet of boats drifted out to sea?" Tina asked Tony.

5

Fold

"Let's do an experiment," said Tony. "We can launch our boats in the tub. Then we can see what might happen to boats in a hurricane."

6

Tony and Tina launched their boats in the tub. The little fleet drifted slowly. Then Tony and Tina launched another fleet. They blew hard to make a strong wind. The boats crashed into each other, and some of them sank!

7

TAKE-HOME BOOK
Just in Time
Use with "Dinosaurs Travel."

Jesse and Trevor Go on a Trip

by Dana Catharine
illustrated by Toni Goffe

Travel Time

Jesse and Trevor played a game and asked riddles on their long car trip. Think of something else that would be fun to do in a car. On a sheet of paper, write a few sentences telling about this game or activity. Share your idea with classmates.

School-Home Connection Ask your child to read *Jesse and Trevor Go on a Trip* to you. Then ask your child to tell about the travel time idea he or she wrote about.

Fold

"I know that," says Jesse. "You are a bicycle, just like my own sturdy bicycle!"

"Look, boys, we're in the city!" said Jesse's dad. "You were having so much fun, you didn't notice that we arrived!"

Jesse and Trevor are good friends. Trevor is going with Jesse to visit Jesse's relatives in the city. "I always have fun in the city," says Jesse. "My relatives said they will take us to skate at the ice palace!"

"I packed my own luggage for the trip,"
Trevor tells Jesse. "It's a good thing our
luggage is not the same. We can tell it
apart by the color."

2

"Here is my riddle," says Trevor. "*You
can go places on me. I have two wheels. I have
a horn or a bell, too. What am I?*"

11

"Mice!" says Trevor. "You are mice!
Now it's my turn."

Jesse and Trevor take their luggage to
the car. Oh, no! They both drop their
luggage!

It's a good thing the luggage is
so sturdy!

Everyone gets into the car and buckles up a seat belt. Then Jesse's Dad begins the drive. It's a good thing that Jesse and Trevor are such good companions. It will be a very long drive!

4

"I want to play a different game," says Jesse. "I will ask a riddle. You figure out the answer. Here is my riddle. *We are very small. We are gray. We squeak. What are we?*"

9

"Let's play a game," says Jesse's mom. "We will count cars for the next five miles."

Jesse counts red cars, Trevor counts blue cars, and Jesse's mom counts trucks. Who counts the most?

"Can we listen to a cassette?" asks Trevor. "I want to hear some music."

"I want to listen to a story cassette," says Jesse. "I don't want music!"

"Are you boys being good companions now?" asks Jesse's mom.

The boys have to make a choice. Will
they listen to music? Will they listen to
a story?

"I know," says Jesse. "We can listen to
music for a little while. Then we can listen
to a story."

The boys are good companions again!

6

While the boys are listening to the
cassettes, they have a snack. Jesse eats an
orange. Trevor eats apple slices and a piece
of cheese.

7

TAKE-HOME BOOK
Just in Time
Use with "Abuela."

Answers: a. 4;   b. 1;   c. 3;   d. 2;   e. 5

Grammy and Me

by Fernando Ruiz
illustrated by Nan Brooks

Fold

What Did You Order?

On a sheet of paper, write the letters *a*, *b*, *c*, *d*, and *e* down the left side. Beside them, write the numbers 1 to 5 to put the pictures in story order. (Turn the page to find the answers.)

a.

b.

c.

d.

e.

 School-Home Connection Ask your child to read *Grammy and Me* to you. Then ask how the girl in the story feels about her grandmother and how your child knows.

Fold

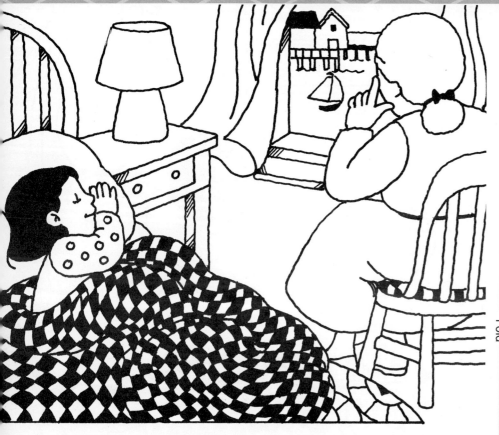

When Grammy finishes her rest, I take mine. I lie quietly in the stillness of Grammy's room while she sings to me as she looks out over the harbor. I love my visits to Grammy's house!

Grammy lives near the harbor. When I have lunch with Grammy, I see small boats and big ships. I see flocks of birds that soar up high and swoop down to find fish.

Every day after lunch, Grammy goes upstairs to take her afternoon rest. She climbs the stairs slowly and carefully.

2

When Grammy gets up from her rest, she always gives me a hug. I think she is glad that I have stayed with her.

11

Sometimes I read to Grammy while she rests. She likes stories about the sea. I read her poems that I write, too. She likes that the best!

Grammy likes to rest in the stillness and darkness of her room. Soon I miss Grammy. I climb the stairs as quietly as a mouse.

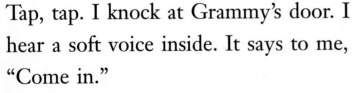

Tap, tap. I knock at Grammy's door. I
hear a soft voice inside. It says to me,
"Come in."

4

Sometimes I play my recorder. I make
music to go with the birds' songs. Grammy
likes my music. Sometimes she hums along.
I like it when Grammy hums. She has a
pretty voice.

9

Sometimes I sit by the open window and watch a flock of birds in the sky. The birds soar up high and then swoop down over the harbor. They do this to spot and catch fish.

8

When I enter, I see Grammy lying on her bed. She looks peaceful and thoughtful. I wonder what pictures are dancing around in her head.

5

Sometimes I play quietly while Grammy rests. I sit on the floor and play with Grammy's buttons. She has a basket full of them. I like to make pictures with the buttons.

6

Sometimes I look out the window and watch the sailboats glide by on the water. Then I look at Grammy. If she is awake, I say softly, "Oh, Grammy, look how gracefully they glide!"

7

TAKE-HOME BOOK
Just in Time
Use with "Ruth Law Thrills a Nation."

Answers: 1. T   2. F   3. T   4. T   5. T   6. F   7. T   8. T

Monarchs to Mexico

by Isabella Cummings
illustrated by Christine Joy Pratt

Monarch Butterfly Facts

On a sheet of paper, write the numbers 1 to 8. Read the sentences in the butterfly. If the sentence tells something true, write a *T*. If the sentence tells something not true, or false, write an *F*. (Turn the page to find the answers.)

1. Some monarch butterflies migrate when they are just two or three weeks old.

2. Monarch butterflies fly north when it gets cold.

3. Monarch butterflies can fly fifty miles in one day.

4. Many monarch butterflies travel to Mexico every year.

5. The wind helps the monarch butterflies fly.

6. Monarch butterflies lose weight when they travel to Mexico.

7. Monarch butterflies get energy from their fat.

8. Monarch butterflies eat nectar.

 School-Home Connection Invite your child to read *Monarchs to Mexico* to you. Then ask your child to tell you three facts he or she learned about monarch butterflies.

The monarch butterflies would stay in Mexico for five or six months. When spring arrived, they would make another amazing trip. They would travel back to their northern homes!

12

It was early fall in North America. At the zoo, the leaves had begun to change color. Spectators came to the zoo to see both the changing leaves and the animals.

1

As the days grew colder, the giraffes and elephants moved inside. The polar bears, however, refused to use their indoor homes. They stood their ground outdoors because they liked the cold.

2

The butterfly heroes and heroines were happy and warm. Far to the north, there were cold winds and snow. In the Mexican mountains, it was cool but not cold. It was perfect for the monarchs.

11

After many weeks, more than one hundred million monarch butterflies arrived in the Mexican mountains. Some of the butterflies returned to the same trees they had lived in the year before!

10

Like the polar bears, many spectators were outside, too. The spectators also stood their ground against the cold. They refused to let cold weather stop them from enjoying the zoo.

3

High in the bright sky, a huge group of monarch butterflies flew over the zoo. The North American winter would be too cold for them. They were off to find hospitality in a warmer place.

4

The butterflies ate nectar from flowers. It is hard to believe, but these butterflies gained weight during their flight! The fat in their bodies gave them energy to fly. The strong winds helped in their flight, too.

9

Fold

The butterflies flew about fifty miles every day. Then they stopped to rest. Some landed on tree branches. Others landed on flowers.

8

Some of the monarch butterflies were only two or three weeks old. But these young heroes and heroines were performing a feat that many animals could not. They were making a trip to Mexico. The butterflies liked the warmer hospitality of the Mexican mountains.

5

Making this migration was quite a feat. Some of the butterflies had to travel more than 1,500 miles.

As the monarch butterflies flew south, others joined them in their migration to Mexico. How many monarchs were in the sky now?

TAKE-HOME BOOK
Just in Time
Use with "Postcards from Pluto."

by David Webb
illustrated by Viki Woodworth

Picnic Time

On a sheet of paper, draw a picture of Carl and Andy. What else might Carl and Andy see at their night picnic? Write a sentence in a speech balloon for each boy. Have him tell something interesting he sees.

 School-Home Connection Ask your child to read *Night Picnic* to you. Then help your child find and name objects in the night sky.

The family quickly packed up and ran to the car. Just when they were safely inside, an intense flash of lightning lit the night sky.

"That lightning was intense," said Andy, "but we are safe in our car. I'm glad we had our picnic before the storm!"

12

Carl and Andy helped get the food ready for their family's picnic. They assembled the sandwiches. Then they gathered the chips, the salad, the watermelon, and the juice. Finally, they put all the food into the picnic basket.

1

Mama, Papa, Carl, and Andy were happy. They were going to the beach at the lake for a picnic. This was not an everyday picnic. It was a picnic at night!

2

Suddenly everyone heard the roar of thunder. "We need to end our night picnic right now," said Papa. "A thunderstorm is approaching. It's dangerous to be near water when there is lightning."

11

Mama assembled some rocks on the
sand. "This is what the Big Dipper and the
Little Dipper look like," she said. "Can you
find them in the sky?"

10

Carl and Andy always enjoyed picnics
at night. Night picnics were very different
from day picnics. Why?

3

Fold

Night picnics were on the beach at the lake. Day picnics were on the boys' front lawn. Carl and Andy had more fun at night because they were at the beach.

"Okay," said Mama. "Papa can be a guide, too. We will lead you on a trip across the sky!"

"Do you see that bright light?" asked Papa, pointing. "That's a planet. You can tell it's not a star because it's not twinkling."

"Will you tell us about the night sky, Mama?" asked Carl. "We can imagine that we are taking a trip across the sky. You can be our guide."

8

The family sat on the beach and enjoyed the picnic dinner. After that, Mama and Papa made a campfire. There was no wind, so it was not dangerous. Then they all lay on their blankets and watched the night sky.

5

"Look at the moon," said Carl. "It's shining so brightly in the sky."

"The moon isn't really shining," said Mama. "It's reflecting the sun's light. That's why it looks so bright."

"I see the moon on the surface of the water, too," said Andy. "Are there two moons?"

"No," answered Papa. "The water reflects light. You are seeing the moon reflected on its surface."